The Learning Resource Center

Hurlbutt Elementary School

HISTORY OPENS WINDOWS

The Ancient Greeks

PAT TAYLOR

Heinemann Interactive Library
Chicago, Illinois

Printed in Hong Kong, China

04 03 02 01
10 9 8 7 6 5 4

The Library of Congress has cataloged
the hardcover version of this book as
follows:
**Library of Congress Cataloging-
in-Publication Data**
Taylor, Pat, 1948-
    The ancient Greeks / Pat Taylor.
    p.   cm. -- (History opens windows)
Includes index.
    Summary: An introduction to various
elements of ancient Greek civilization
including gods and goddesses, clothing,
food, town and country life, art and
theater, and the Olympic games.
ISBN 0-431-05704-4 (lib. bind.)
    1. Greece--Civilization--To 146 B.C.--
Juvenile literature.   [1. Greece--
Civilization--To 146 B.C.]   I. Title.
II. Series.
DF77.T35   1997
938--DC21   96-53223
                                CIP
                                AC

Paperback ISBN 1-57572-589-4

Acknowledgments
The author and publishers are grateful to the following for
permission to reproduce copyright photographs:
Photographers' Library, p. 7; Michael Holford, pp. 9, 15;
H.L. Pierce Fund, Museum of Fine Arts, Boston, p. 10; Sonia
Halliday Photographs, pp. 22, 25; Ancient Art and
Architecture Collection/Ronald Sheridan, pp. 24, 29.

Cover photo © British Museum, London

Contents

Introduction

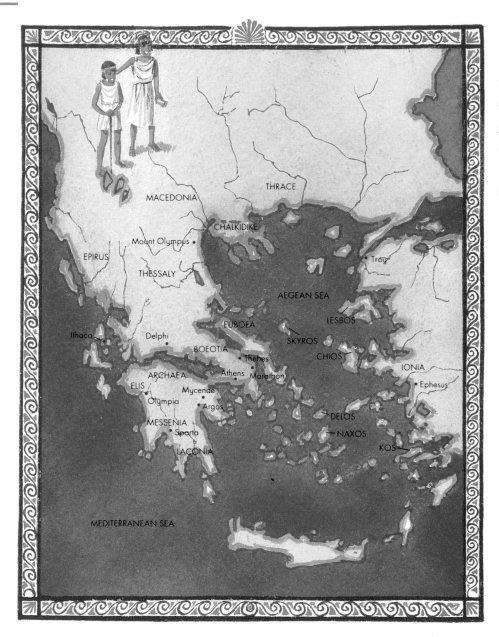

Greece is a rocky country. Many of its people live near the sea. There are many islands.

			Alexander the Great 356–323 B.C.
Egyptians	The first Greeks	Dark Ages	ANCIENT GREECE
2000 B.C.	1100 B.C.	800 B.C.	146 B.C.

People lived in Greece from earliest times. Different groups of people organized their lives in different ways. They did not think of themselves as Greeks. By 800 B.C., villages began to grow into towns. Some of the Greeks made city states. They traded with each other and with other countries. Some of the city states like Athens became very rich. Much of the evidence we have from Ancient Greece is from Athens. The people made beautiful vase paintings and statues. They wrote stories, poems, and plays. They knew about science and math. We still use many of their ideas. Some of the letters of our alphabet come from Greek letters.

Sometimes the city states fought each other. Sometimes they fought together against other countries. In 499 B.C. they started to fight against Persia. Alexander the Great ruled all of Greece, but when he died his land was split up. The Romans took control of Greece in 146 B.C. You can see this marked on the time line below.

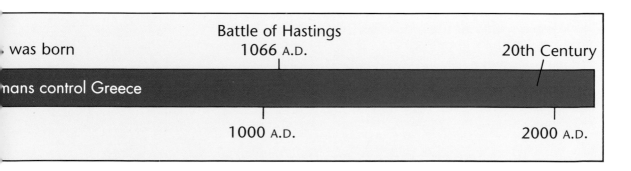

Battle of Hastings
1066 A.D.

was born

20th Century

mans control Greece

1000 A.D.

2000 A.D.

Gods and goddesses

The Greeks believed in many gods and goddesses. They controlled everything, from the weather to the way people felt. The Greeks thought that some of them lived on Mount Olympus. There are many stories about Greek gods and goddesses which we can read today.

These are some of the Greek gods and goddesses.

Hermes
Messenger of the gods.

Zeus
The most important god.

Hera
Wife of Zeus and queen of heaven.

Apollo
God of music. People went to his temple if they wanted to know about the future.

Athene
Goddess of wisdom.

The Greeks built temples in every town. Each temple was for a particular god or goddess. People went to the temple to pray. Sometimes they took a gift to please the god. If this was an animal the priest would sacrifice (kill) it.

One temple still standing today is the Parthenon. It is in Athens and was built for the goddess Athene.

This is the Parthenon. It had an enormous statue of Athene in it.

Clothes

Greek people wore loose clothes because Greece is a warm country. We can tell what they wore from their vase paintings and statues. Most people wore a tunic called a chiton. It was made from two rectangular pieces of cloth with holes for head and arms. Girls and boys dressed alike in short chitons. Men and women wore long ones. The Greeks also wore a cloak called a himation.

This is a Greek family with their slaves.

The Greek woman sitting down is having a necklace put on her. This scene is from a vase painting.

Rich people's clothes were made of wool or linen. Sometimes their clothes were brightly colored. They wore boots or sandals. The women wore makeup. On special occasions women may have worn a fine wig.

Poor people and slaves did not wear shoes. Their clothes were usually made from wool.

Food

The Greeks ate a variety of foods. They enjoyed a lot of fish. They only had big pieces of meat at festivals. More often they ate small birds like thrushes and swallows. In addition to meats, the Greeks had lentils, radishes, celery, and beans. They ate cheese, cakes, and fruit. The women, or their slaves, ground grain to make flour and bread. They made wine from grapes.

Many Greeks lived by the sea and caught fish to eat. We can see from this vase painting that they used a rod and line. They also used pots to catch lobsters.

Men and women did not eat meals together. The men lay on couches and were given the food by slaves. They had plates made from pottery. They ate with a metal spoon and knife or with their fingers. There was often music and dancing after the meal. Women and children usually ate together.

Some men at a dinner party.

Children

In most parts of Ancient Greece, boys were seen as more important than girls. Boys whose families could afford it started school when they were six. They learned to read, add, and write and to enjoy poetry and music.

The girls helped their mothers around the house. They would cook, weave, and clean. Some were taught to read and write by their mothers. In Sparta, girls went to school and learned to be fit and strong.

This boy is learning how to write.

12

We know that when children died they were buried with their toys. These toys have been uncovered.

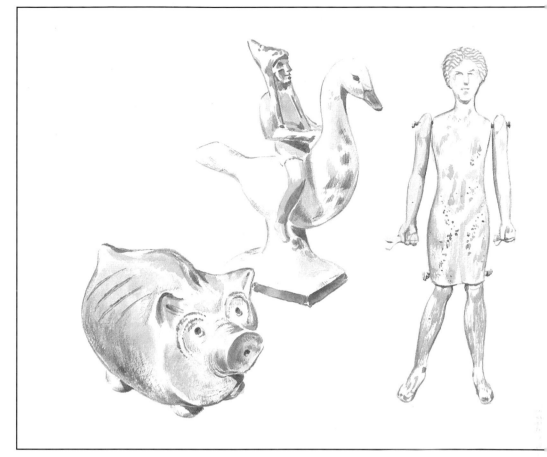

Greek children played with toys that were made of clay or leather.

When they turned 15, Greek girls threw away their toys and married men chosen by their fathers.

When they turned 16, Athenian boys trained for jobs, perhaps as craftsmen. At age 18 they became citizens and could vote. Slaves and women, however, were not allowed to vote.

Health and illness

The Ancient Greeks tried to keep fit and well. They thought that the gods made them ill. If they became ill they went to sleep near the temple of the god Asclepius. They thought that this would make them better. They also made medicine from plants.

This person is sleeping near the temple of Asclepius to try to get better.

These are tools that Greek doctors used. The cup was used to catch blood. The saw was used to cut off legs and arms. The tweezers were used to pull out spearheads. The spoon was for giving medicine.

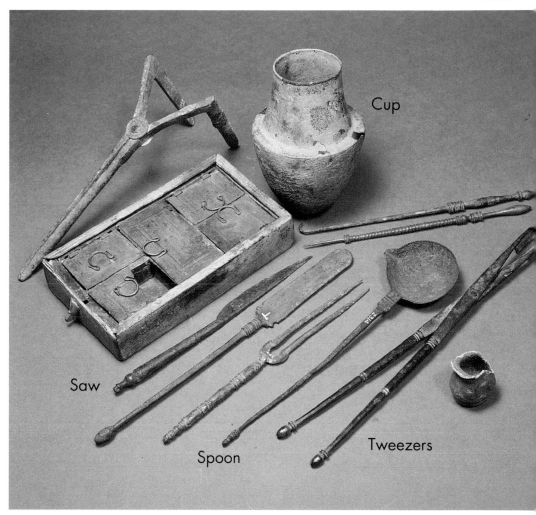

Cup

Saw

Spoon

Tweezers

Greek doctors had new ideas about why a person became ill. The most famous of these doctors was Hippocrates. He did not think that illness came from the gods. His ideas about how a doctor should work still affect us today.

Buildings

Some Greek buildings still stand today. These were the buildings that everybody used and saw as important. Many of them took years to build. Stones had to be carried on wagons from the quarries. They were lifted by ropes and pulleys and held together with small pieces of wood and metal.

Many Greek buildings had columns to hold up their roofs. There are three types of columns: Doric, Ionic and Corinthian.

Houses were made of mud bricks. They were not built to last. Poor people's houses were very simple. Rich people's houses had more rooms. They were built around a courtyard. There were large, cool rooms but not much furniture. Men and women had their own rooms.

Doric

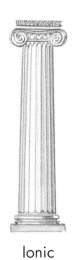

Ionic

Corinthian

The first columns that the Greeks built were plain. Later they decorated them more.

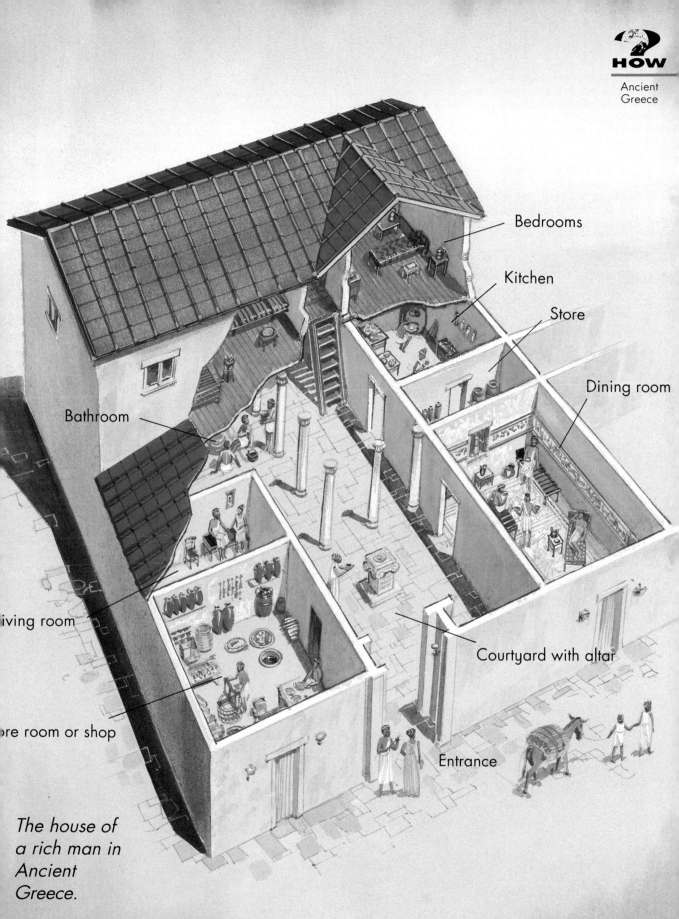

Bedrooms

Kitchen

Store

Dining room

Bathroom

Living room

Store room or shop

Courtyard with altar

Entrance

*The house of
a rich man in
Ancient
Greece.*

Town life

Ancient Greece was divided into small areas called city states. Only Athens and Sparta were big. Each city state had its own laws. Sometimes it had its own coins and army. At its center was a town with a fortified hill called an acropolis.

Athens was a democracy. This means that every man born in Athens, unless he was a slave, could vote on how the city state was run.

Not guilty

Guilty

These disks were used in the law courts. They would decide if a person was guilty or not guilty.

In the middle of the town was the agora. This is where the main buildings were. It was also a meeting place. There were bankers' stalls, market stalls, and law courts. People would walk around and chat. There schoolboys, acrobats and musicians, and slaves for sale. Around the agora were the town houses. Craftsmen lived in these houses. The fronts of their houses were their workshops.

The agora
was a very
busy place in
a Greek
town.

Trade and ships

The Ancient Greeks traded with other
countries such as Egypt, Syria and Sicily.
The Greeks found it easier to travel by sea
than over land because of the mountains
and poor roads. The Greeks could find
where they were going by the stars. They
built merchant ships to carry their goods.
The ships carried slaves, wood,
corn, iron and copper.

*At first the
Greeks
bartered
(swapped)
their goods.
Later, some
city-states
had their
own coins.
This is the
'owl' of
Athens.*

Leather ropes

Linen sail

Hull

Bow

Ram

Painted eye to keep evil spiri
away or for the ship to see w
it was going

The merchant ships were made of wood and had a large hold to store the cargo. They had a sail and oars. They were slow and heavy but there were other Greek ships which were lighter. These were warships called triremes. In peacetime they could protect the merchant ships from pirates. They had a ram to hit other ships. They had three rows of oarsmen and could carry 200 men.

This is a trireme.

—— Stern

—— Steering oar

Country life

Most Greek people lived in the country and were farmers. It was a hard life. The soil was rocky and did not grow very good crops. It rained too much in the winter and too little in the summer. The summer was also very hot.

Grapes grew on the sides of the hills. Olive trees grew on the poor soil, just as they do today. On the better soil, the Greeks grew corn. They also raised donkeys, sheep, and goats.

This is what Greece looks like now. It has not changed much since the time of the Ancient Greeks. It is a hot, dry, and rocky place.

Here are some people at work in the country. You can see that the women and children had to work.

The roads were very poor and most people walked. Some people had horses and carts and rich people rode on horseback. As well as farmers there were carpenters to make and mend carts. There were herdsmen to look after the animals. There were also miners who dug for silver.

The Olympic Games

The Greeks liked sports. We think that the Olympic Games began in 776 B.C. They were held in Olympia every four years.

The Games were part of Greek religious life. They started with a sacrifice to Zeus. Some events, like chariot racing, are not in the Games today. Other events, like the pentathlon, still are. To win the pentathlon, athletes had to complete five events: discus throwing, javelin throwing, wrestling, running, and long jumping. Winners of all races were given olive wreaths to wear on their heads.

This is a famous statue of a discus thrower. A Greek discus was a flat metal plate.

This is a Greek stadium. The athletes ran one or two stades. A stade was about 656 feet. The spectators sat on the stone seats.

Olympia had a stadium, baths and temples. We can still see the remains of some of these buildings.

The Olympic Games were stopped by the emperor Theodosius in 393 A.D. Then, in 1896, they were started again. Today there are Winter and Summer Games, held every four years. The Games begin when an athlete lights a special flame with a torch brought from Olympia.

Art and theater

The Ancient Greeks enjoyed all kinds of art. They liked paintings, music, poems, and statues. Their vase paintings and statues tell us what they did and what they looked like. The statues took a long time to make and were usually painted. We do not know what their music sounded like. But we know from vase paintings that they played harps and pipes.

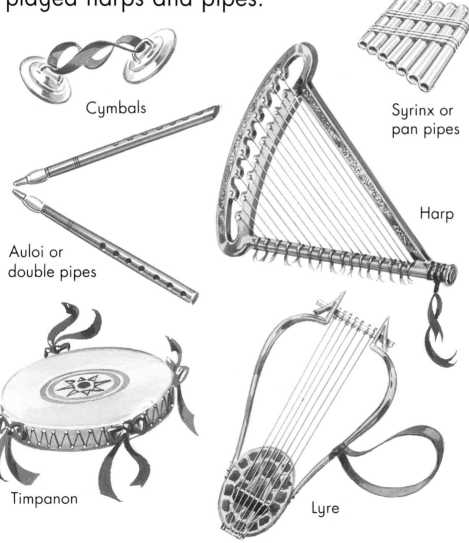

Cymbals

Syrinx or pan pipes

Harp

Auloi or double pipes

Timpanon

Lyre

We know that the Greeks had all these instruments. We can see them in vase paintings.

Greek plays are still performed today. This one is in an Ancient Greek theater.

Many Greek towns had an open-air theater. These theaters were only used for festivals. People watched about four plays, one after the other. The plays were either funny (comedies) or sad (tragedies). All the actors were men. They had to play more than one part. They wore masks to show who they were playing.

Great thinkers

The Greeks wanted to know about their world. Was it flat? What happened to the sun at night? Where were the stars in the day time? They would sit in the agora and talk, telling each other of their ideas. They wanted to know about water. Archimedes discovered why it overflowed and how to move it uphill.

This is the screw that Archimedes invented to bring water uphill.

Plato

Socrates

Herodotus

These are statues of famous Greeks.

Some Greeks, like Pythagoras, studied math and looked at shapes and angles. Some, like Socrates, wondered what made people behave the way they did. And some thought about good and evil. Some, like Plato, thought about how countries should be ruled. Herodotus studied history. We can learn a lot about the Greeks from his writings.

29

Famous stories

We know lots of stories about Greek people. Some of these stories were made up around things that really happened. There really was a war between Greece and Troy. The stories that are told about the war in a book called *The Iliad* may not be true, but they are famous.

This shows how the Greeks captured the city of Troy. The story is told in The Iliad.

We know much more about Alexander the Great. He was taught by Aristotle, an important thinker. Alexander the Great ruled Greece after his father Philip died. He won many battles and took over many lands. He later ruled Egypt and built a large city called Alexandria. After he died, all his land was split up. It was later taken by the Romans.

This is a picture of Alexander the Great. It was made out of small pieces of colored tiles. It is called a mosaic.

Index

*Please note that Athene can also be spelled Athena.

32